We Can See Three

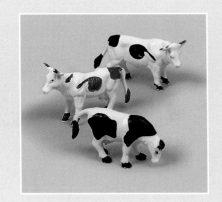

3 three :·

Here is a little farm.

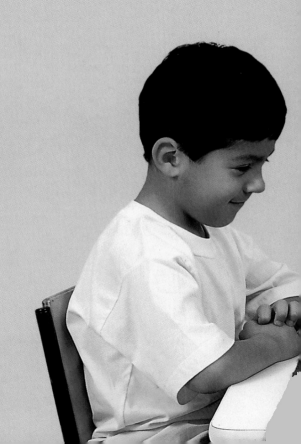

3

Look! Here are three horses

for the farm.

3 horses

The horses can go here.

One, two, three horses.

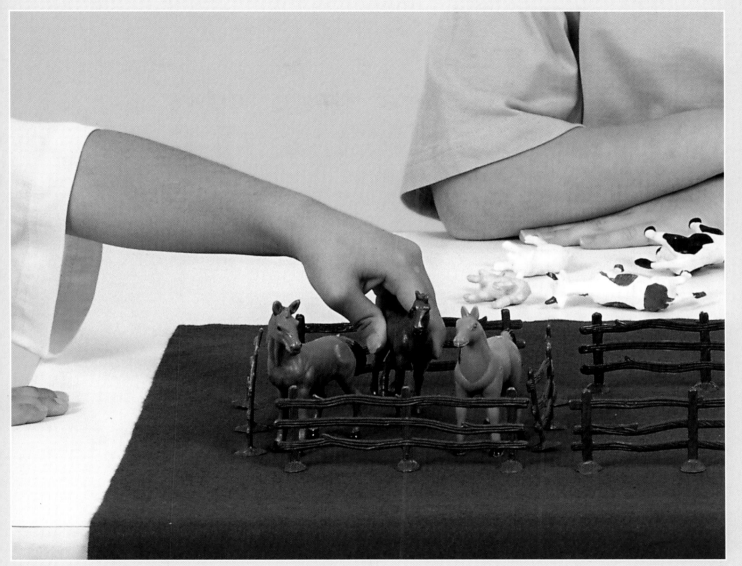

And here are three cows

for the farm.

3 cows

The cows can go here.

One, two, three cows.

And here are three sheep

for the farm.

3   sheep

The sheep can go here.

One, two, three sheep.

Look at the little farm.

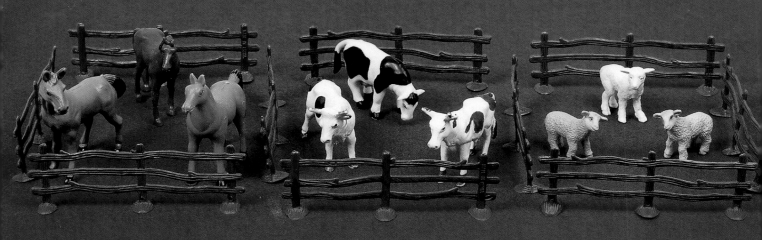

three horses   three cows   three sheep